I'm an Activist

By Wil Mara

Senior Editors Satu Hämeenaho-Fox, Roohi Sehgal
Editorial Assistant Abi Luscombe
Project Art Editors Emma Hobson, Kanika Kalra Grover
Jacket Coordinator Issy Walsh
Jacket Designer Katie Knutton
DTP Designers Vijay Kandwal, Dheeraj Singh
Picture Researchers Sakshi Saluja, Nimesh Agrawal
Producer, Pre-Production Dragana Puvacic
Senior Producer Ena Matagic
Managing Editors Laura Gilbert, Monica Saigal
Managing Art Editor Diane Peyton Jones
Deputy Managing Art Editor Ivy Sengupta
Delhi Team Head Malavika Talukder
Creative Director Helen Senior
Publishing Director Sarah Larter

Reading Consultant Jacqueline Harris
Subject Consultant Dr Simin Fadaee

First published in Great Britain in 2019 by
Dorling Kindersley Limited
80 Strand, London, WC2R 0RL

Copyright © 2019 Dorling Kindersley Limited
A Penguin Random House Company
10 9 8 7 6 5 4 3 2 1
001–314602–Nov/2019

A CIP catalogue record for this book
is available from the British Library.
ISBN: 978-0-2413-8625-5

Printed and bound in China

The publisher would like to thank the following for their kind permission to reproduce their photographs:
(Key: a-above; b-below/bottom; c-centre; f-far; l-left; r-right; t-top)

1 Getty Images: Central Press. **3 Alamy Stock Photo:** WENN Rights Ltd (br). **5 Getty Images:** PHAS / UIG. **6 Getty Images:** Peter Skingley / Bride Lane Library / Popperfoto (b). **7 Alamy Stock Photo:** Raj Singh (t). **8 Library of Congress, Washington, D.C.:** Harvey Lindsley / LC-DIG-ppmsca-54232 (bl). **9 Alamy Stock Photo:** Granger Historical Picture Archive (t). **10 Getty Images:** Rice / Library of Congress / Corbis / VCG. **11 Getty Images:** Library of Congress / Corbis / VCG (tr). **12 Alamy Stock Photo:** Pictorial Press Ltd (t). **13 Getty Images:** George Rinhart / Corbis (b). **14 Alamy Stock Photo:** PictureLux / The Hollywood Archive (bl). **15 Getty Images:** Underwood Archives (t). **16–17 Getty Images:** Central Press. **18 Alamy Stock Photo:** Dinodia Photos. **21 Getty Images:** Kevin Carter / Sygma. **22 Alamy Stock Photo:** Peter Righteous (c). **Getty Images:** Christophel Fine Art / UIG (br). **23 Getty Images:** (t); Michael Reaves (cb). **24 Getty Images:** Fotosearch (bl). **25 Alamy Stock Photo:** Kim Petersen (t). **26–27 Alamy Stock Photo:** Trinity Mirror / Mirrorpix (b). **29 Alamy Stock Photo:** Canary Islands. **30 Alamy Stock Photo:** David Halbakken (t). **31 Getty Images:** K M Asad / LightRocket. **32–33 Getty Images:** Esref Musa / Anadolu Agency (t). **33 Getty Images:** Safin Hamed / AFP (cr). **34 Rex by Shutterstock:** Sandy Schaeffer Hopkins / Shutterstock (t). **34–35 Getty Images:** Noam Galai / Wirelmage. **37 Getty Images:** Alfred Eisenstaedt / The LIFE Picture Collection. **38–39 Getty Images:** Sebastian Gollnow / AFP. **40 Alamy Stock Photo:** WENN Rights Ltd (t). **41 Dreamstime.com:** Sharon Day / Shaday365 (br). **42–43 Getty Images:** Andia / UIG (b). **44 Getty Images:** Hanna Franzen / AFP. **46 Alamy Stock Photo:** Sueddeutsche Zeitung Photo (bc). **Getty Images:** Gallo Images (cl). **47 Alamy Stock Photo:** Historic Images (tl). **Dreamstime.com:** Bravissimos (bl/Swirl). **Getty Images:** David Redfern / Redferns (c); John Rodgers / Redferns (bl). **49 Rex by Shutterstock:** Patrick Lewis / Starpix / Shutterstock. **50 Alamy Stock Photo:** Shelly Rivoli / Alamy Live News (bl). **51 Getty Images:** Matt McClain / The Washington Post. **52 Getty Images:** Jay Directo / AFP. **54 Alamy Stock Photo:** Historic Collection (clb); White House Photo (cr). **54–55 Dreamstime.com:** Simon Gurney / Donsimon (Background). **55 Alamy Stock Photo:** The History Collection (cr); Jack Abuin / ZUMAPRESS.com (tl). **Getty Images:** Paul Morigi / Wirelmage (bl). **56 Alamy Stock Photo:** Jackie Ellis (cr). **56–57 Getty Images:** PangeaSeed Foundation / Barcroft / Barcroft Media (b/Mural). **57 Alamy Stock Photo:** Danny Callcut / Alamy Live News (t); The Protected Art Archive (crb/Gulliver's Travels). **Depositphotos Inc:** Rangizzz (crb). **63 Getty Images:** Matt McClain / The Washington Post (br)
Endpaper images: *Front*: **Getty Images:** Kevin Carter / Sygma; *Back*: **Getty Images:** Kevin Carter / Sygma

Cover images: *Front*: **123RF.com:** Volodymyr Melnyk cb, Photka c, Starsstudio clb; **iStockphoto.com:** Michaeljung c/ (Girl holding white board); *Back*: **Getty Images:** Jim Watson / AFP tr

All other images © Dorling Kindersley
For further information see: www.dkimages.com

A WORLD OF IDEAS:
SEE ALL THERE IS TO KNOW
www.dk.com

Contents

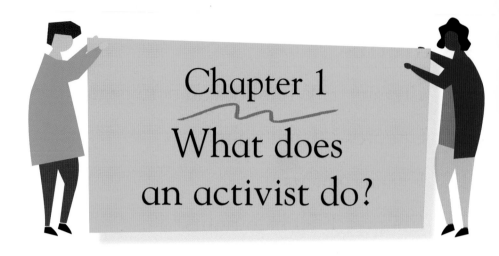

Chapter 1

What does an activist do?

An activist is someone who takes action to help solve important problems in the world. An activist is willing to stand up for what they believe in, in order to reach a certain goal.

One early activist was the ancient Roman Spartacus. After being captured in war, he inspired fellow enslaved people to escape and start a rebellion. Another early activist was a French girl named Joan of Arc (1412–1431). She led a French army to victory in a war against England. Joan was later captured and killed for this.

Joan of Arc leading French soldiers into battle against the English.

5

In the 19th century, more people started to work in cities. Even children worked in factories and workshops. Conditions were very bad. People were often hurt by the machines or got ill from chemicals or coal dust. Workers joined together to protest against the way they were treated. They went on strike (refused to work) until they got better treatment and pay.

The people of Brighton, UK, showing their support for the miners' strike in September 1984.

A group of women peacefully demonstrating for women's rights in Bangalore (now Bengaluru), India, in 2009.

In the 20th century, activists fought for equal rights between all people. Women wanted to be treated equally to men. Gay people wanted to be able to live without discrimination. Racist systems such as the South African apartheid were ended after protests organized by activists.

One of the greatest problems in early American history was slavery. This was the practice of "owning" another person in order to make them work for no pay. By the 1800s, many people were taking action against slavery. These people were called "abolitionists".

One well-known abolitionist was a woman named Sojourner Truth. She was born into slavery but escaped to freedom when she was very young.

Then she travelled the country giving speeches against slavery.

Harriet Tubman was another dedicated abolitionist. She helped at least 70 people escape slavery using the

Harriet Tubman

Underground Railroad.

The Underground Railroad had stops where people fleeing slavery were given food and directions to safe places.

This was a secret network of paths and houses that brought enslaved people safely to the northern United States and Canada where slavery was against the law.

Susan B. Anthony (*centre*) founded the International Council of Women.

An ongoing issue in the world is women's rights. It is the struggle of girls and women to be treated the same as men in all ways. For centuries, women were not allowed to do all sorts of things, such as own property or run

The Suffrage Movement communicated through their newspaper, *The Revolution.*

for public office. Over time, however, activists known as feminists began fighting for gender equality. American Susan B. Anthony, for example, founded many feminist organizations in the 1800s. She also helped start a pro-women newspaper called *The Revolution.* There was also Alice Paul, another American, who was the leader of a women's political group called the National Woman's Party.

Women gathered at the Suffrage headquarters
in Cleveland, Ohio, USA, in 1912.

Many feminists were part of
the Suffrage Movement. This was the
struggle to gain women the right
to vote. In the early 1900s, women
in the USA were not allowed to
vote for people running for public
office. The Suffragists fought this
in court. They organized marches.

The US Congress finally granted women the right to vote by adopting the 19th Amendment to the Constitution in 1920.

In Great Britain, suffragette Emmeline Pankhurst was known for her sometimes violent approach to the cause. However, her actions did help force the British Government to give women over the age of 21 the right to vote in 1928.

Emmeline Pankhurst (*second from left*) leading protesters along Victoria Embankment, London, in 1915.

Chapter 2
Civil rights

On 5 December 1955, Rosa Parks was sitting on a bus in Montgomery, Alabama. There was a rule that any black person had to give up their seat to a white person if the bus got full. When some white people got on the bus that day, the driver told Rosa to move. She refused, and she was arrested.

Rosa Parks said she was "tired of giving in" to racism.

Rosa Parks was fingerprinted during her arrest for refusing to give up her seat to a white passenger.

After this, thousands of black people in the area stopped riding the buses. The story became news all around the country. The bus company soon changed their rule about black people having to give up their seats.

Dr Martin Luther King, Jr. was one of the most important activists in history. As a young man, he was a church minister in Montgomery, Alabama. He was known for his excellent skills at public speaking. After the arrest of Rosa Parks, he led the Montgomery bus boycott. This was part of a "non-violent" way to get to equal rights. It meant he and his followers refused to hurt anyone or damage anything they owned.

King became very famous in the years that followed and helped create new civil rights laws. Sadly, he was murdered by a gunman on 4 April 1968, in Memphis, Tennessee.

Dr Martin Luther King, Jr. leads the 1963 March on Washington, protesting the injustices faced by African-Americans.

Mahatma Gandhi and his followers during a march against British taxes in Dandi, India, 1930.

India-born Mahatma Gandhi also took the non-violent approach to civil rights. In his youth, he realized that Indians were treated terribly in many places around the world. The nation of India itself was under the control of another nation (Great Britain). Gandhi spent his adult life working for the freedom of the Indian people. He made speeches, took legal action and worked with politicians. India finally became an independent country in 1947. Gandhi was murdered by a gunman one year later.

Born in South Africa in 1918, Nelson Mandela was always very angry about a system called "apartheid". This was a rule that kept people of different skin colours separate in South Africa. It also made life better for rich white people over everyone else. Mandela and his followers tried to get rid of their government in 1962. Mandela was caught and sentenced to life in prison. However, he was released in 1990 and continued his war against apartheid. Then South Africa held its first political election where people of different skin colours were allowed to vote and run for office. Mandela became president and kept fighting apartheid until the end of his life. He died in 2013 after a long illness.

Nelson Mandela, like Gandhi and Dr King, believed in non-violence. He hoped that the South African Government would change its unfair ways.

Famous protests

There are many famous examples of protests throughout history. These have inspired similar protests all around the world.

Protestant Reformation
In 1517, a monk named Martin Luther said that people should honour the Bible and not the Pope. Thousands agreed and began leaving the Catholic Church.

The Boston Tea Party, USA
On 16 December 1773, Boston colonists boarded ships and threw all the tea overboard. They were angry about British tea taxes!

The Arab Spring
By late 2010, many people in Middle Eastern countries were tired of being poor. So they began a huge protest against their governments.

US National Anthem Protests
Some American athletes refuse to stand during the national anthem. Called "taking a knee", this is in protest of the harsh treatment of minorities by police.

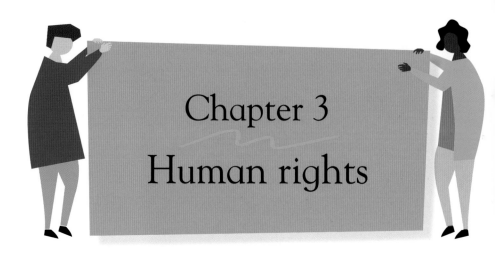

Chapter 3
Human rights

The Universal Declaration of Human Rights was written by the United Nations (UN) in 1948. The UN is a group that works to keep the peace between the countries of the world.

Eleanor Roosevelt with a copy of the Universal Declaration of Human Rights in 1949.

The European headquarters of the United Nations in Geneva, Switzerland.

The Declaration says that all people must be allowed certain freedoms. For example, all people have the right to a religion of their choice. All people have the right to be treated the same. Everyone has the right to basic needs, such as food, clothing and a place to live.

LGBT+ people include those who are gay, lesbian, bisexual or trans. In the past, gay people have been treated very badly. They have been insulted. They have been the target of extreme acts of violence.

Actors Ian McKellen and Michael Cashman, and gays rights activist Peter Tatchell lead a march in Manchester, UK, in 1988.

They have often been unable to find jobs. They have not been able to be open about who they fall in love with.

The rights of LGBT+ people have improved in recent times. For example, laws have been passed in many countries making it a crime to refuse someone a job just because they're gay.

In 2001, the Netherlands became the first country to legalize same-sex marriage. Other countries have since followed suit. However, there are still many places around the world where LGBT+ people are treated badly.

A participant at a gay pride march in Maspalomas, Spain, in 2014.

A clothes factory in Phnom Penh, Cambodia.

In some parts of the world, people who work in factories have few rights. The "textile" business (making clothes) has millions of workers. Sadly, many of them work in dangerous conditions. In some factories, people are not paid for extra hours that they work. If they become angry about this, they are fired. Women who get pregnant often lose their job.

Textile workers protesting during a Labour Day rally in Dhaka, Bangladesh, on 1 May 2016.

31

A bird's-eye view of a refugee camp in Idlib, Syria, in 2018.

Human rights problems often occur during a refugee crisis. This is when a large number of people leave a certain place because it has become too dangerous. One of the biggest refugee crises today started in Syria. Syria's civil war began in 2011. Millions of Syrian people fled to other countries.

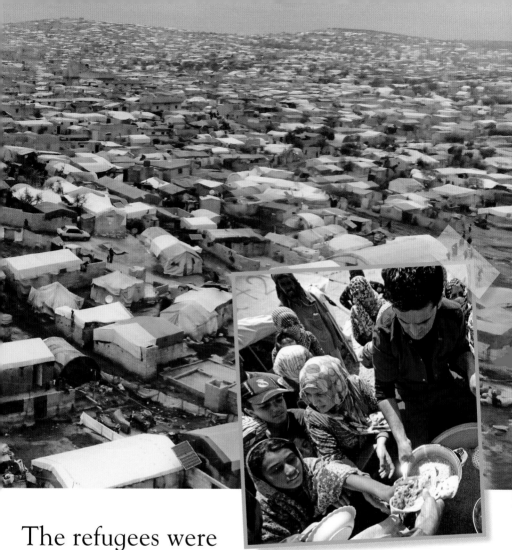

Syrian women queue up for food at Quru Gusik refugee camp in Arbil, Iraq.

The refugees were then treated very poorly. They were often refused basic needs, such as food, water and housing. Many refugees still live in tents, in huge temporary camps.

In 2015, when she was just five, Sophie told the Pope about her campaign.

Sophie Cruz

Sophie makes speeches asking for help for immigrants who don't yet have the legal right to live in the USA, such as her parents. She has spoken with powerful people, from presidents to the Pope.

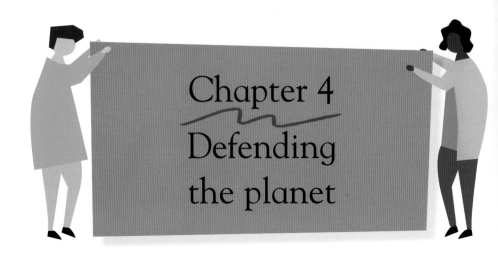

Chapter 4
Defending the planet

Rachel Carson was an American scientist who loved nature. By the 1950s, she was writing books and articles about it. One of the things that worried her was chemicals. These were being used by companies to kill off pests that eat crops. However, they were also hurting other plants and animals. Rachel wrote a book about this problem in 1962, called *Silent Spring*. The book became very popular and changed the way the public looked at nature. It started a form of activism called the environmental movement.

Rachel Carson spent decades studying nature, including in the woods near her home.

One of the most important organizations to come out of the environmental movement is Greenpeace. It was set up by Irving and Dorothy Stowe in 1971. One of Greenpeace's main goals was to make sure businesses didn't do things to harm the environment. For example, some companies dumped their rubbish into the oceans. Greenpeace made sure the public knew about these actions. In time, more and more people supported Greenpeace. Today, it is able to work with the leaders of many governments.

Greenpeace activists campaign against pollution from diesel cars in Stuttgart, Germany, 2018.

Children gather in London to protest against the ivory trade in 2015.

Because of human actions, animals such as elephants are in danger. Elephants are found in both Africa and Asia, usually in open grasslands and forests. Most people think elephants are beautiful creatures. Others, however, trap and kill elephants for different reasons.

One is to take their tusks, which are made of ivory. They can sell the tusks for a great deal of money. Some people hunt elephants just for fun. Fortunately, there are more organizations than ever before working to protect elephants. One approach is to persuade governments to make laws against elephant hunting.

Many elephants are still being illegally hunted despite a ban on the ivory trade.

Activists can reach the public through "grassroots" work. For example, they talk to ordinary people directly or send out letters. They want the public to learn more about problems facing the world. One is the protection of land. Natural land offers important things to all of us, such as fresh air and clean water.

However, some people want to destroy land for their own reasons. For example, a large area of land may be needed to build a shopping centre or an office. Land activists work with the people who will be most affected – those who live there.

Indonesian farmers protest against companies taking their land to grow oil palms in Sumatra, Indonesia.

Greta Thunberg at her climate change protest holding a poster saying, "School strike for climate change".

Greta Thunberg (2003–) is a climate activist from Sweden. She gained worldwide attention after inspiring children across the globe to protest against climate change. Thunberg first learned about climate change when she was eight years old. At the time, she could not believe that adults didn't seem to care.

At the age of 15, Thunberg decided to act. Every day, she sat outside the Swedish parliament building. Her goal was to make the government pay attention to climate change, and take action to stop it. Since then, Thunberg has given speeches around the world, including at the United Nations.

Protest songs

Music is a popular way of spreading protest messages. Some very famous artists have written and performed protest songs.

Miriam Makeba, South Africa
Makeba was a singer and songwriter. Many of her songs were about apartheid and the unfair practices of her government.

Bruce Springsteen, USA
Springsteen's parents worked hard but had little money. When he began writing songs, his lyrics were often about the struggles of working-class people.

Bankim C. Chatterjee, India

Chatterjee's poem "Vande Mataram" became the national song of India when it was trying to gain independence from Britain.

Joan Baez, USA

Baez is a folk singer who has performed hundreds of protest songs. Most are about civil rights, peace between nations or the environment.

John Lennon, UK

Lennon wrote protest songs both as a member of the group The Beatles and as a solo artist. Some of the issues he covered included human rights and war.

Chapter 5
Children's rights

While still a teenager, Malala Yousafzai made big changes in the education of young women. She began writing a blog in 2009 about how the Taliban – an extremist religious group – didn't let girls get an education in Pakistan's Swat Valley. *The New York Times* wrote a story about Malala. The article got attention all around the world. A Taliban gunman tried to kill her on 12 October 2012. Malala survived, and continues to work for girls' education. In 2014, she became the youngest-ever winner of the Nobel Peace Prize.

Malala Yousafzai at the premiere of the film *He Named Me Malala* in New York, USA, 2015.

On 14 February 2018, 17 students and staff were killed in a mass shooting at Marjory Stoneman Douglas High School in Florida, USA. One of the students who survived was Emma González. Emma became angry at the many politicians who didn't push for greater gun control following the shooting. She started a group called "Never Again MSD" along with 19 other students. In 2018, Never Again forced Florida politicians to pass stronger gun laws. Many people saw this as a huge win over the National Rifle Association, which has powerful political connections.

A supporter at a rally in 2018 holding a poster with the words, "My kids are more important than your guns".

Emma González (*centre*)
with fellow students at
the "March for Our Lives"
on 24 March 2018.

Children in Manila, the Philippines, celebrating children's rights during a parade in 2008. Their sign reads "Stop child abuse now".

In 1989, the United Nations created an agreement to protect children's rights. This is called the Convention on the Rights of the Child. Almost every country in the world has signed the agreement. It has helped to improve the lives of children around the world.

New rights have been added since 1989 – for example, digital rights. This means that children deserve to be protected from harmful websites and videos. As the world changes, we must all fight for new rights to help us live healthy, happy lives.

Children's rights advocates

Many activists have devoted their lives to making sure the world's children are as safe, happy and educated as possible.

Edith Dircksey Cowan, Australia

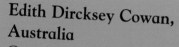

Cowan founded the Children's Protection Society in 1906. She wanted children to have better schooling, medical care and legal rights.

Michelle Obama, USA
As First Lady, Michelle Obama worried about child obesity. She encouraged children to eat healthy foods and get plenty of exercise.

Florence Kelley, USA
Born in 1859, Kelley spent her life improving conditions for children who were sent out to work.

Princess Madeleine of Sweden
Madeleine helps to raise awareness of the World Childhood Foundation. The Foundation works to stop children from being treated badly.

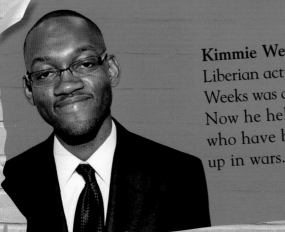

Kimmie Weeks, Liberia
Liberian activist Kimmie Weeks was a child refugee. Now he helps children who have been caught up in wars.

Surprising approaches

Protesting isn't just about marching or making speeches. There are all sorts of ways to take part in a worthy cause!

Artivism
Awareness of important issues can be spread through various art forms. Types of artivism include live performances and street paintings.

Dustbin art opposing drilling for gas in South Africa.

Craftivism

Craftivism is the creation of crafts for protest. Hand-made works are made and shown to draw attention to issues such as the environment.

Written satire

Satire mocks the bad behaviour of powerful people. Jonathan Swift's book *Gulliver's Travels* is about the poor way people treat one another in society.

Artist Aaron Glasson created a mural to highlight threats to oceans and marine life.

Quiz

1. Which secret network did Harriet Tubman use to help people escape slavery?

2. What year were British women over the age of 21 given the right to vote?

3. What did Rosa Parks refuse to do?

4. In what year did India become an independent country?

5. What was the racist political system in South Africa called?

6. What was the huge 2010 protest in the Middle East called?

7   Which organization wrote the Universal Declaration of Human Rights?

8   Which country was the first to legalize same-sex marriage?

9   What was Rachel Carson's influential book about the environment called?

10   Which animals are hunted for their tusks, which are made of ivory?

11   Who was the youngest ever winner of the Nobel Peace Prize in 2014?

12   What is the name for activism that includes paintings and performances?

Answers on page 61

Glossary

abuse
physical and verbal harm

apartheid
separating people by the colour of their skin

boycott
refuse to visit a place or buy from a company
to show you disagree with its actions

civil rights
laws that make sure everyone is treated fairly

civil war
war between groups in the same country

colonist
person who represents a country that controls
other countries

discrimination
treating someone unfairly due to the group
they come from, for example, another race

election
event where a group of people vote for
their leaders

independent country
country that is not controlled by another country

minority group
group of people who are different in some way
(for example, race or religion) from most other
people in the place they live

peace
period where there is no war or fighting between countries

protest
to disapprove of something and fight for it to change

racism
discriminating against people from other races

rally
large group of people meeting to show support for a cause

suffragettes
activists who took direct action to get women the
right to vote

suffragists
activists who peacefully worked to get women the
right to vote

Answers to the quiz:
1. The Underground Railroad; **2**. 1928; **3**. Give up her seat on
the bus to a white person; **4**. 1947; **5**. Apartheid; **6**. The Arab
Spring; **7**. The United Nations; **8**.The Netherlands; **9**. *Silent
Spring*; **10**. Elephants; **11**. Malala Yousafzai; **12**. Artivism

Index

A LEVEL FOR EVERY READER

This book is a part of an exciting four-level reading series to support children in developing the habit of reading widely for both pleasure and information. Each book is designed to develop a child's reading skills, fluency, grammar awareness and comprehension in order to build confidence and enjoyment when reading.

Ready for a Level 3 (Beginning to Read Alone) book
A child should:
- be able to read many words without needing to stop and break them down into sound parts.
- read smoothly, in phrases and with expression and at a good pace.
- self-correct when a word or sentence doesn't sound right or doesn't make sense.

A valuable and shared reading experience
For many children, reading requires much effort, but adult participation can make reading both fun and easier. Here are a few tips on how to use this book with a young reader:

Check out the contents together:
- read about the book on the back cover and talk about the contents page to help heighten interest and expectation.
- ask the reader to make predictions about what they think will happen next.
- talk about the information he/she might want to find out.

Encourage fluent reading:
- encourage reading aloud in fluent, expressive phrases, making full use of punctuation and thinking about the meaning; if helpful, choose a sentence to read aloud to help demonstrate reading with expression.

Praise, share and talk:
- notice if the reader is responding to the text by self-correcting and varying his/her voice.
- encourage the reader to recall specific details after each chapter.
- let him/her pick out interesting words and discuss what they mean.
- talk about what he/she found most interesting or important and show your own enthusiasm for the book.
- read the quiz at the end of the book and encourage the reader to answer the questions, if necessary, by turning back to the relevant pages to find the answers.